THE PET SHOW

by Judy Nayer
Illustrated by Marisol Sarrazin

Modern Curriculum Press

Computer colorizations by Lucie Maragni

Cover and book design by Agatha Jaspon

ISBN 0-7652-1362-1

Printed in the United States of America

6 7 8 9 10 11 12 13   07 06 05 04 03 02

Modern
Curriculum
Press

Pearson Learning Group

1-800-321-3106
www.pearsonlearning.com

Contents

For Matthew, with love

Chapter 1
Red Rescue

Andy turned off the TV. He had just finished watching *The Red Rescue Show*. It was one of the few TV shows he watched.

Red Rescue was a big red dog who was very brave. He was always saving someone. Once he saved a boy from a fire. Another time he found a little girl who was lost.

Andy loved *The Red Rescue Show*. He dreamed of having a dog like Red. That would never happen. Andy would never have a dog like Red.

Andy's dad was allergic to dogs. Dog fur made him sneeze. He sneezed at cat fur, rabbit fur, and gerbil fur. Even bird feathers made his dad sneeze.

Andy would never have a dog. It wasn't fair. That's the way it was.

Chapter 2
The Pet Show

"I'll go talk to Zack," Andy thought. His friend always listened to Andy's problems.

"Mom!" he called. "I'm going to Zack's."

He heard her yell, "Have fun!" Then he put on his jacket and went out the door.

Andy Lopez and Zack Gibson lived next to each other on B Street. Andy saw Zack putting a sign on his little sister's bike. Zack's dog Henry was chewing on a bone.

"Did you see *Red Rescue*?" asked Andy.

"Oh, no!" Zack said. "I missed *Red Rescue*. I forgot what time it was."

Andy patted Henry. "I wish I could have a pet like Red Rescue or Henry," he said.

"How about a goldfish?" Zack asked. He knew why Andy couldn't have a furry pet.

Andy looked glum. "No, thanks," he said. Andy didn't want a fish. A fish wasn't a good pet. You couldn't hold a fish or pet it.

Andy looked down at the newspaper Zack had put on the ground. He saw a big ad. It read:

PET SHOW
Saturday April 15th. 11 A.M.
Bring your pet to Lakeland School gym.
Your pet could win a prize.
Meet TV dog Red Rescue!

"Zack!" yelled Andy. "Look at this! It says we can meet Red Rescue!" He picked up the newspaper to show Zack.

Andy was excited. Then he stopped. How could he enter a pet show without a pet? If he couldn't go to the pet show, he couldn't meet Red Rescue. Andy just *had* to have a pet! He had only two days to find one.

Chapter 3
Everyone's Pets

The next day, Andy walked to school with Zack and their friends Lisa Hira and Katy Stone. They all lived on B Street. As they walked, they talked about the pet show.

"My cat will win," Lisa said proudly.

"My gerbils are the best pets," Katy said. "They can do tricks."

Andy thought about how lucky the others were. They all had pets.

Zack was the luckiest. He had his big dog Henry. Lisa had a fluffy white cat named Snowball. Katy had gerbils. At first, she had just two. Then the gerbils had babies. Now Katy had lots of gerbils.

When they got to school, everyone in class was talking about the pet show.

"I'm bringing my parrot," said Pete.

"I'm bringing my rabbit," said Ann.

"I'm bringing my ant farm," said Keesha.

"How about you, Andy?" asked Dean. "Are you bringing a pet to the pet show?"

Andy sighed. "I don't have a pet."

Katy felt sorry for Andy. "Do you want to borrow one of my gerbils?" she asked. "You can take Bo. He does the best tricks. You can have the maze I made for him."

"Maybe you could rent a pet," Lisa said. She always had a way to fix problems.

"No, thanks," said Andy. He wanted a pet of his own.

Soon Ms. Rivers, their teacher, said it was reading time. Everyone had to pick a book and read at their desks. Andy went over to the basket that said "Animals." He got a book called *All About Snakes.* He read:

Many people are afraid of snakes. Most snakes are harmless. Only a few snakes are poisonous.

The book had a map. The map showed a lot of snakes where Andy lived. None of these snakes was poisonous.

Andy liked the book about snakes, but it was hard to keep his mind on reading. He kept thinking about the pet show.

Everyone was going to the pet show with their pets. Andy just had to get a pet of his own. He had to think of something!

Chapter 4
Surprise at the Lake

Andy took the long way home with
Zack. They went through Lakeland Park.
Soon they came to the lake. Andy walked
near the water.

Just then Andy saw something jump out of the lake. It was a frog!

"Look at that," he said to Zack. "Maybe I can have a frog for a pet. A frog doesn't have feathers. A frog doesn't have fur. A frog won't make my dad sneeze."

Andy tried to grab the frog, but it was too jumpy. It hopped into the water before Andy could get it. Zack laughed.

"I have to go home. Good luck with your frog," Zack said. He walked on toward B Street.

Andy tried to catch the frog again, but the frog swam away. Then Andy saw something else move. This time it was in the grass. Andy bent down and looked. He saw two small, shiny eyes. It was a snake!

Andy jumped back. He almost ran.
Then he remembered what he had read.
There were no poisonous snakes where
he lived.

The snake was hardly moving. It was
green and skinny and long. It looked
harmless. It even looked friendly.

Andy took out the book about snakes he had brought with him from school. He flipped through the pages. He found a picture of a snake that looked just like the snake he had found. The book said it wasn't at all poisonous.

Andy wondered if a snake would be a
good pet. Andy put his backpack on the
ground. He opened it and stepped away.
He would let the snake decide.

The snake seemed curious. It crawled
right into Andy's backpack. "I guess you do
want to be my pet," said Andy.

Chapter 5
Andy's Pet

Andy picked up his backpack. The snake tumbled down to the bottom. Andy zipped the backpack closed. Then he ran the rest of the way home.

Andy went straight to his garage. He found a cardboard box. He poked air holes in the lid. He found some sand and some sticks. He put them in the box. Then he filled a small bowl with water. He put that in the box, too.

Andy held the backpack upside down over the open box. The snake slid out. It began to crawl around the box.

Andy put his hand in the box. "I'll try to find you a better home," he said.

Then he touched the snake. It wasn't slimy. It was dry and smooth.

Andy took out the book and read more. His snake ate spiders, insects, and worms.

"Ugh," thought Andy. Where would he get bugs? Then he looked up. Spiders! He knew this kind was harmless, too. Andy caught one. He put it in the box.

"Here you go," said Andy.

The snake moved fast. Snap! The spider was gone.

"Andy! Dinner!" his mom called. Andy
put the lid on the box and left the garage.

After dinner, Andy called Zack.

"Zack, I have a pet," Andy said quickly.

"Did you catch the frog?" asked Zack.

"No, it's a snake," Andy said.

"A snake!" Zack cried.

"He's harmless," Andy said. "I've named him Sammy. I don't really know how to take care of him. You have a pet. Can you keep him for me until the show tomorrow?"

"No, I don't know anything about snakes," Zack said.

Lisa said the same thing when Andy called her. At last, Katy said she would take the snake. Her brother had an old tank he used when he had a pet turtle.

Andy hurried over to Katy's house. "I'll pick him up tomorrow before the show," he said. At last, Andy had a pet!

Chapter 6
The Big Day

Andy got up very early the next day. It was Saturday, the day of the pet show.

Andy went to Katy's house. She was up early, too. "I'll see you at the show," Katy said as she handed Sammy to Andy.

Andy asked his mom if he could go to the pet show with Zack and his dad. He did not say anything about Sammy. Andy's mom told him that he could go.

The pet show was crowded. There were
animals everywhere. Lisa carried Snowball.
Katy held a cage with four gerbils in it.
There were birds, fish, mice, lots of dogs,
turtles, rabbits, and even a pig.

35

Everyone stood in line. They were
waiting to show their pets to the judges.
Andy saw Red Rescue on the stage!

Pete showed his parrot. It kept saying,
"Hello, Red." The judges liked that.

At last it was Andy's turn. He opened the
box. Oh, no! Sammy was gone!

Chapter 7
On the Loose

Andy heard a scream. Someone yelled, "It's a. . . a. . . snake!"

Then everyone started screaming. Cats meowed. Dogs barked. Birds squawked. A duck quacked. The pig grunted. Pete's parrot flew off, shouting, "Snake! Snake!"

Snowball jumped out of Lisa's hands and
went after the parrot. Henry pulled loose
from Zack and chased Snowball.

Andy dropped the box. He ran to find
Sammy. Someone might step on him!

Andy saw a snake's tail move around someone's leg. He turned. He tripped over the pig and almost stepped on a cat.

Then Andy heard Red Rescue bark. Red was staring at something.

It was Sammy! Andy ran over
to Sammy. He gently picked him up
behind his head. The crowd became quiet.

"It's okay, everybody," said Andy. "It's
only Sammy. He's my pet."

"Wow!" someone said. "I didn't know
Andy had a snake!"

"That was so cool!" said Zack. "You really know how to handle him."

All the pets found their owners after Andy put Sammy in his box. The pet show went on.

In the end, everyone got a prize. Zack's dog Henry got the prize for Biggest Pet. Lisa's cat Snowball won Fluffiest Pet. Katy's gerbils were the Busiest Pets. Sammy was the Most Unusual Pet!

Andy finally got to meet Red Rescue. He even had his picture taken with Red.

Now what was he going to do with Sammy? Andy still had not told his parents about his new pet.

Chapter 8
Andy's New Pet

When Andy got home from the show, he showed his mom the prize he had won.

"What is this for?" she asked.

Andy opened the box and showed her Sammy. "He's my new pet," Andy said.

His mom said Sammy was nice, but he came from the wild. Andy had to put him back in the wild.

The next day, Zack, Lisa, Katy, and Andy took Sammy back to the park.

Andy said good-bye. He said he would visit Sammy soon.

At home, Andy said, "I really want a pet. Is there anything we can do?"

"Maybe there is," his mom and dad said.

They got in the car. Andy was surprised when they parked in front of the pet store.

Andy picked out a pet. He thought about getting a snake like Sammy. Then he saw something else that wouldn't make his dad sneeze. It was even better than a snake.

Andy finally had a pet of his own. It was a pet iguana. Andy named him Lucky. He felt pretty lucky to have him. Best of all, Lucky liked to eat vegetables, not bugs.

Glossary

allergic   [uh LUR jihk] can be made sick by breathing in or touching something that doesn't hurt most people

curious   [KYOOR ee us] wanting to find out about something

handle   [HAN dul] hold or use with hands

harmless   [HAHRM lus] cannot hurt

judges   [JUHJ uz] people who choose a winner

maze   [mayz] winding walkway that is hard to find a way through

poisonous   [POY zun us] something that can hurt or kill

slimy   [SLYE mee] covered with something slick or slipper